The Ba
(and other people like)

Ed Hambleton

GILEAD
B O O K S

Gilead Books Publishing
Corner Farm
West Knapton
Malton
North Yorkshire YO17 8JB UK
www.GileadBooksPublishing.com

First published in Great Britain, October 2012
2 4 6 8 10 9 7 5 3 1

Copyright © Ed Hambleton 2012

British Library Cataloguing-in-Publication Data:
A catalogue record for this book is available from the British
Library.

ISBN-13: 978-0-9568560-6-7

The publisher makes every effort to ensure that the papers used
in our books are made from trees that have been legally sourced
from well-managed and credibly certified forests by using a
printer awarded FSC & PEFC chain of custody certification.

Cover illustration: Anna Tash
Design: Nathan Ward

To Laura and Katy Grace

∞

Acknowledgements

In writing this book special thanks must go to the following people:

- Chris Hayes, Dave Burton and all at Gilead Books for their help in bringing this project to publication.

- Carl Beech for his excellent foreword.

- The numerous friends and family who have offered invaluable wisdom, advice and constructive criticism during the entirety of this project.

- To my dear wife Laura who, as with everything I do, has been my strongest supporter and most loving critic.

- Finally, to the hero of this book, Jesus Christ, the man who was born to reach me, lived to teach me, died to save me, rose to give me new life, ascended to Heaven to prepare a home for me, and is seated next to God praying for me. This is for You.

Foreword

People are asking questions. They want to know what it's all about. I know this because I try to point people to the answers for my living. Because of this, I'm always on the lookout for something that will help people. What Ed has done with this book is drill down, in seven concise chapters, into some of the big questions people might have when they are considering what it means to follow Jesus. So I'm guessing that if you have this book in your hand you are either one of two situations. 1) You're a person with questions or 2) you know someone who's asking them! My advice is this; if you are one of the questioners, then you need to read past this foreword and give this book a go over a couple of mugs of your favourite brew. It won't take you forever to read it; in fact it won't take you long at all. But it will get you thinking. Similarly, if you know someone with questions, then buy this book and give it to them as a gift. Then follow it up with a conversation. Seven chapters, seven key issues, and just a bit of your time required.

So how about it? If Jesus is who he claims to be then that's a game changer! That's got to be worth spending just a bit of your life looking into, hasn't it? Enjoy the read!

Carl Beech
General Director of Christian Vision for Men (CVM) an International Christian Men's Movement

Contents

Introduction
John 1:43-51

We were sat in a dusty old church hall on a cold, wet, windy November evening. My co-group leader and I looked around the ten or so people who had been assigned to our group. To say that it was an eclectic mix of folk would have been an understatement. We had a range of different ages, backgrounds, nationalities and opinions, and as the conversations got going we soon learnt that there were further differences hidden beneath the surface. Each person had a story of how they had ended up there on that November evening. Some were straight out of university, having turned their backs on the church when the shackles of parental guidance had been loosened. Now graduated, they wanted to explore the belief system again to see if it held water. A young couple with a baby sat opposite me, holding hands. They wanted to provide a secure home for their new arrival, and wondered if the church had any advice that might be useful. Further round to the right was a much older lady, a churchgoer by tradition who had never really been convinced that she actually believed the things she heard every week, and wanted the chance to discuss the claims of the Bible rationally. Further to the right again, another woman of a similar age, who hadn't attended a church for decades and who was wholly convinced that Christianity held little - if any - relevance for today, but who was attending to appease a Christian friend who had invited her.

By way of trying to gauge the audience further and focus our conversations, I sent out a starter for ten.

"So, who do you think Jesus was?"

After a few seconds of awkward silence the answers started to come back in, with the irregularity that might have been expected from such a diverse group. Prophet. Magician. Teacher. Saviour. Good example. Fictional character. Guardian angel. Fortune-teller. Friend. At the time the range of answers took me by surprise, but since then I've realised that the answers that night actually showed a good cross-section of society at large.

Over the past two thousand years, our perceptions of Jesus have undergone some serious makeovers. We all recognise the classic Westernised representation of Jesus; Caucasian, long beard, flowing locks; clean, tidy and more than a little effeminate. But is this an accurate portrayal of the man we read about in Sunday School? From the age of twelve to thirty he would have been working with his father Joseph in a carpenter's shop. The hands that were to be punctured by Roman nails would have been calloused and splintered, not finely manicured like they are in the films. After years of manual labour he would probably have had considerable upper body strength and cut an imposing, muscular figure.

Each and every society is guilty. We have turned Jesus into a respectable, unchallenging, easy-to-stomach image in order to suit our needs. However, as we look into the eyewitness accounts, we begin to discover what Jesus was really like, not what Hollywood has turned him into.

It seems that everyone has a different opinion of who Jesus was and what he came to do. He has been reduced to a relative concept, who can be interpreted any which way you choose. This isn't a recent phenomenon either. As we read the pages of the Bible, it becomes clear that there was as much dispute about who Jesus was when he walked on earth as there is now. The stories of Jesus recorded by Matthew, Mark, Luke and John show us that during his ministry people tried to dismiss Jesus, downplay him, questioned his sanity and even suggested that he was possessed by the Devil (Mark 8:48).

At the start of his public life, Jesus called together twelve followers – the men we call disciples. One of these men, Philip, was so impressed with Jesus that he went and told his friend Nathanael that he had found God's Messiah, and that he was living just a few miles away in Nazareth. Nathanael, as anyone would be, was highly sceptical. He had his own idea of what God should be like, and by the sound of things Jesus didn't measure up. Instead of trying to prove Nathanael wrong, Philip had a much better solution; an invitation to come and meet Jesus for himself and make his own mind up. No clever arguments, no small print, just three simple words. Come and see.

No one comes to God as a neutral. We all come with thoughts and opinions that we have picked up through our lives, whether from the things we have been taught or the experiences we have gone through. When we approach God we come with questions, doubts and fears. Jesus is God's way of giving us some answers. Nathanael came to see the evidence and came to his own conclusions. The Bible is our chance to put our preconceptions to one side, read the eyewitness accounts and make our own mind up – to ask if Jesus really was who he claimed to be.

Back to the cold church hall in November. Once the hubbub of the first question had died down, I offered a second question to the group: What do you think Jesus would say to you if he met you face to face?

This time the responses came back with much more uniformity. There was a consensus that Jesus would be angry, disappointed and disapproving. And why?

We've let him down. We're not good enough. Deep down people are still very religious. They think that there are a series of divine hoops to be jumped through and boxes to be ticked and – like some kind of driving test – if you can get through life without getting more than fifteen minors or one major then you'll be OK. And I think that, further down, people also have a nagging feeling that they've messed things up already. But is that what God is like? Does He shut the door in people's faces and put up a "No Entry" sign if we've broken a few key rules? Is that what Jesus was like?

People often assume that the Bible is merely a collection of outdated rules and implausible stories, but in actual fact it is all about relationships. It contains practical advice on how husbands and wives should love one another and make marriage work, how parents and children should live in harmony and how bosses and employees should treat one another (Ephesians 5:21 – 6:9). More than that, though, it is a story about our relationship with God, how that relationship has been broken, and how through Jesus we can be brought back to God.

The Bible tells us that Jesus, despite being born as a human, was also God (Colossians 2:9). Jesus was like us in so many ways. If he didn't eat he was hungry, if he didn't drink he was thirsty, if he had a long day he felt tired, and if something upset him he cried. However, the Bible also claims that Jesus was more than just a man; that the baby born in a manger in Bethlehem was God himself living on earth in human form (Matthew 1:23). If we want to know what God is like then all we have to do is look at Jesus (John 14:9).

During his time on earth Jesus met with all kinds of people - people of different genders, ethnicities, ages, education and wealth. Through the stories of Jesus we can see how he would interact with people like us. Each story is different, and often very surprising. Jesus didn't come to earth with a manifesto or a well-rehearsed sales pitch, but he tailored his message of hope to suit each individual hearer, the situation they were in and the issues that mattered to them most.

The message of the Bible, the message of Jesus, is that God saw the mess that we were in and the mistakes we all make and didn't turn His back on us. In Jesus he came to be in our situation and offer a solution. He came to meet people like you and me. If you want to know what that looks like, then read on and see what unexpected things happen when God comes to town. What would Jesus really say if he met you face to face? Come and see.

MORALITY

∞

Jesus and the Rich Young Man
Matthew 19:16-30

Our first visit to the stories of Jesus finds us eavesdropping on a conversation between Jesus and a "rich young man". Although we don't know this man's name, the story is recorded in three of the gospels (Matthew, Mark and Luke), and from a few key clues in the text we can learn quite a lot about him. All three writers refer to him as being "of great wealth", Matthew refers to him as being young, and Luke refers to him as being a ruler. He is probably from a wealthy background, and he is almost certainly well educated and successful. He has risen through the ranks of society quickly and is probably a well-known leader in the local community. Given the conversation he has with Jesus, it is obvious that he is a moral and upright member of society who has attended plenty of religious services. However, from his opening question to Jesus ("Teacher, what good thing must I do to get eternal life?"), it is clear that despite all his good deeds he is still unsure whether or not he is quite good enough to get into Heaven.

Just like the rich young man in this story, many people in the UK don't live in poverty (at least globally speaking), are of the respectable type, and know a bit about religion from Sunday School or RE lessons. At the very least they might go to church for the occasional Christmas or Easter service. Most people also like to think that they are "good". Yes, they might have committed the odd misdemeanour here or there, but none of the big stuff. I've not had an affair, I don't steal, I've not killed anyone and I give to charity... is that enough? Do I pass? And yet much of society has the same anxiety that the rich young man had when he approached Jesus; we are worried that God has a standard and we're not sure if we're above or below the line. We like to think that the benchmark is placed somewhere beneath us and that we have our heads above the water. At the bottom of the pile are the usual suspects: Adolf Hitler, Josef Stalin and Pol Pot, to name just a few. At the top of the list are people like Mother Teresa and Gandhi, and we like to place ourselves somewhere just above middle. But how can we be sure?

That is why the rich young man came to find Jesus. He wanted to know if there was anything he could do that would drag him above the line for sure, anything that would tip the balance in his favour and guarantee him a place in Heaven. He knows that he isn't *really* bad, but will God think that he's *really* good? How can any of us know for certain that we've done enough to get into Heaven?

Oscar Wilde's novel, *The Picture of Dorian Gray*, is the story of a young man who had it all. He was young, charming and devastatingly handsome. After posing as a model for an artist, Dorian becomes envious of a painting of himself when he realises that the picture will be beautiful forever while his own looks will wither and fade with the passing years. He passionately wishes that it could be the other way around. Dorian's wish is granted, and over the coming decades the painting, which is locked in his attic, receives the marks of a debauched lifestyle and a malicious soul but Dorian himself remains youthful and elegant. After years of excessive living and immoral behaviour Dorian becomes ashamed of his life as it is shown on his secret painting and turns to altruism. After a few acts of kindness he climbs the stairs to once again view his portrait. To his dismay the painting is no better off. His moral efforts couldn't erase what had already past and he is confronted with a hideous reminder of what his life has really looked like.

God has seen the painting in our attic. Our friends, colleagues and families might be impressed with outward appearances but God knows what we are really like. He knows every white lie we have told, every secret thought and every evil deed, no matter how large or how small. Good deeds are to be applauded and encouraged, but they can't paint over a multitude of sins. However much we try to change the painting in our attic through changing our behaviour, we can't erase the mistakes we've made. Only Jesus can do that for us. He can replace our disfigured painting with one of exquisite beauty.

If we were all given one question to ask God, most people would probably want to know whether they're going to make it to Heaven. When he was asked this question by the rich young man, Jesus initially replied that in order to get to Heaven he must obey the commandments. The rich young man was happy with the response Jesus gave him – he felt that he had been able to keep these commandments since he was a child (elsewhere Jesus teaches that in fact nobody has been able to keep all of the commandments (Matthew 5:22; 5:28ff). However, he still didn't feel sure that he had done quite enough, and so asked again, "What do I still lack?"

This time Jesus gave him a very different response: "If you want to be perfect, go and sell your possessions and give them to the poor, and you will have treasure in Heaven. Then come, follow me."

When the young man heard this he went away sad, because he had great wealth. The rich young man had lived a good life but Jesus wanted more from him than just a few acts of kindness. He wanted the man's heart. You can't serve God and money, and the rich young man had to make a choice between the two.

In July 2007 a woman was arrested for contempt of court. She had been listening to her iPod during a trial. The woman wasn't simply in the public gallery, though – she was a member of the jury. Furthermore, this wasn't just any court case, it was a murder trial. The judge, court officials and fellow jurors were all amazed at the woman's complete disregard for the seriousness of the situation and she was promptly dismissed from the jury.

When you sit on a jury nothing is more important than listening to the evidence that is presented to you. Everything else pales into insignificance and only the most negligent person would allow their attention to go elsewhere. What God wanted from the rich young man is the same as what he wants from us; He wants us to turn our backs on the things that have taken our attention away from Him (whether money or something else). These may be good things or bad things, but at the end of the day it doesn't matter what it is that has become our reason for living. Nothing is more important than being right with God, and if something else has taken our attention away from God then He wants us to rearrange our priorities.

The rich young man had many good intentions. He had tried to reach God in the best way he knew, by behaving as well as he possibly could. He had done many good things but they could not earn him a place in Heaven. At the end of the day the rich young man failed the only test that ever really mattered; will you give your heart to Jesus or to something else?

Jesus wants to be our only Lord, and he's not willing to compete with our bank account, or any other thing we might want to place in front of him. Does this mean that if we want to be a Christian we have to hand over all of our money? The answer is definitely not. There is nothing wrong with being a Christian and owning possessions. The problem is when our possessions begin to own us. God wants to be our top priority, and for the rich young man that was going to be a difficult choice to make.

As the rich young man walked away disappointed at the thought of having to sacrifice his wealth and status for God, the disciples and Jesus carried on their conversation. Jesus remarked that it is easier for a camel to go through the eye of a needle than for a rich man to enter the kingdom of God. "Who then can be saved?" the disciples asked. Jesus looked at them and said, "With man this is impossible, but with God all things are possible." It is impossible for anyone to enter Heaven by trying to be good enough. Instead God wants us to accept Jesus as Lord of our lives and to live to follow him. For some people, such as the rich young man, this is a very difficult decision to make due to all the things they have to give up. Not all of us will have all the wealth and status that the rich young man enjoyed, but we are all given the same choice to make; will we accept Jesus and follow him, or will we put our trust in something else, hoping that our good deeds will be enough to please God and get us into Heaven?

Jesus' message to the rich young man is just as significant today as it was all those years ago. The message is that you cannot gain approval from God by impressing him with your actions and by being a law-abiding citizen.

In your case it might not be wealth that is stopping you from making a commitment to God. Whatever sacrifices you have to make, though, Jesus makes it clear that it will all be worth it in the end. As our first story draws to a close, the disciples asked Jesus what was in it for them. They had done what Jesus had asked and left everything for him, so how would they be rewarded? Jesus answered that for everything they had left for his sake they would be repaid a hundredfold both in this life and the next. Jesus calls us to make sacrifices to follow him, but he promises that following him will always be worth it, no matter what we have to give up.

We don't get to hear the end of the story about the rich young man. As he walked away from Jesus he had a decision to make. I hope that he realised that his best efforts to please God could never earn him eternal life and that the one thing he needed to do was to give God his whole heart. I hope that when he got home and looked round his opulent house he realised that it held a lot of emptiness and dissatisfaction. I hope he realised that owning all the possessions in the world would mean nothing if he lost his soul. I hope he did sell up, give his money to the poor and chase after Jesus with a passion to follow him wherever he went. And I hope that through reading this short story you can realise that you have exactly the same decision to make. Are you floating along in the comfort of wealth and respectability and a few random acts of kindness, hoping that it's going to be enough to pass the test one day? Are you going to answer Jesus' call to leave everything and follow him?

RELIGION

∞

Jesus and Nicodemus
John 3:1-15

The next stop in our journey through the gospels is in John Chapter Three. We find ourselves in Jerusalem at the time of the Passover Feast. Jesus had performed some miraculous signs which had caught the attention of the crowd. It also hadn't escaped the notice of a man called Nicodemus. Nicodemus was a Pharisee. The Pharisees were the most religious of all people, and they championed strict adherence to the laws of the Old Testament. Many of the Pharisees were also Scribes. The Scribes were experts in the Old Testament, and their job was to make sure that the rest of Jewish society were keeping to the rules that had been set all those years before. In order to do this the Scribes devised many additional rules, regulations and rituals, which covered every area of life to make sure that people didn't fall foul of the smallest standard. This often resulted in normal people feeling inferior and inadequate.

If the life of Jesus was a pantomime then the Pharisees would be the villains of the piece. They enter stage left with a sinister look on their faces, accompanied by a minor chord from the orchestra pit. They immediately set about trying to trip Jesus up, catch him out, and they even plotting to kill him (Matthew 12:14). Jesus was almost always in confrontation with the Scribes and the Pharisees, often criticising their hypocritical lifestyles (Matthew 23:13). However, as a group they did have some redeeming features. They were people who were genuinely seeking God, but they had got badly confused along the way – lost in a cloud of traditions, rules and rituals. They had become more interested in trying to look impressive in front of others than loving people and telling them about God (Matthew 23:28).

But when Nicodemus approached Jesus he didn't come with ulterior motives, or with the intention of trying to make Jesus look foolish in front of the watching crowd. Instead he came to Jesus under the cover of darkness and respectfully addressed him as "Teacher". As a teacher of the law he was probably embarrassed that he needed to ask Jesus, a lowly carpenter, a few questions, and he may well have been worried about what the other Scribes and Pharisees would think about him visiting Jesus. But whatever pressures he was feeling, he cast them aside and came to find Jesus. He had seen something in Jesus that made him sit up and take note. There was something different about him, and Nicodemus had to find out what it was.

In the first chapter we saw the rich young man discover that trying to live a moral life wasn't enough on its own to be accepted by God. Would Nicodemus receive a better answer from Jesus? After all, Nicodemus was a devoutly religious man who had devoted his life to studying the Old Testament. However, after Nicodemus' short introduction, Jesus abruptly told him "I tell you the truth, no-one can see the kingdom of God unless he is born again." Jesus wasn't interested in Nicodemus' hours of studying and religious observance. According to Jesus, all of Nicodemus' efforts at being religious were worthless unless he has been "born again".

Jesus was saying to Nicodemus that he was not impressed with his religious fervour or racial identity. What Nicodemus really needed in order to be accepted by God was a fresh start and a new identity. In the same way that the rich young man couldn't change his identity through moral living, neither could Nicodemus change his identity through religious rituals.

Like many people today, Nicodemus didn't understand what it meant to be "born again", so Jesus went on to explain things in more depth. "I tell you the truth, no-one can enter the Kingdom of God unless he is born [again].

Flesh gives birth to flesh, but the Spirit gives birth to spirit." When Jesus talks about "flesh" he is referring to our human identity and efforts. We can try all we like to work our way into an acceptable state before God through morals (like the rich young man) or religion (like Nicodemus), but at the end of the day the only way we can be accepted by God is by having a new identity, and this can't be done by human effort. The Pharisees found this message especially hard to accept, as they were very proud of their religious efforts and their cultural heritage, and assumed that this would guarantee them a place in Heaven (Matthew 3:9). Instead, Jesus taught that only a spiritual rebirth would allow someone to enter Heaven.

I can never read the story of Nicodemus without being transported back into the wonderful world of Narnia, brought to us by the genius of C.S. Lewis. In one scene from The Voyage of the Dawn Treader[1], Eustace slips away from the rest of the party, and after getting quite lost he stumbles on a dragon's lair full of treasure. Eustace fills his pockets with diamonds, slips a gold bracelet over his wrist and falls asleep on his new found mountain of plunder. Upon waking he is horrified to find that he has been turned into a dragon. The thing that changes Eustace back into a boy again is his encounter with Aslan, the Great Lion. Aslan leads Eustace

---

[1] *The Voyage of the Dawn Treader*, C.S. Lewis, HarperCollins (1952)

the Dragon away into the mountains one night, and commands him to "undress". Eustace uses his dragon claws to peel off his scaly skin, only to find that there is yet more scaly skin underneath. He tries again, and again, and finally gives up. However often he tries to change back into a boy he somehow can't manage it on his own. Aslan watches Eustace toil for a while, then stops him. It looks like, he says, Eustace will have to let Aslan do it for him. Aslan moves towards Eustace the Dragon and places a claw into him. The pain is awful. Eustace experiences pain worse than he's ever felt before, and Aslan's claws feel like they've gone right to his heart. But at the same time comes the pleasure of feeling this massive, hardened skin pull away. Eustace can move freely – he becomes a boy again. Aslan then cleans Eustace and gives him new clothes, and Eustace is changed from being arrogant and spiteful into something very different – a new person.

Nicodemus had a lot in common with Eustace. He had tried to change his identity but had failed miserably. Religion had let him down and when he met Jesus he was given a life changing message: If you want to go to Heaven then you will need a fresh start. Religion won't get you anywhere; you need to let me do it for you.

Most people would say that what God must love most of all is people being religious, but the story of Nicodemus shows that this isn't the case. The Bible actually teaches that God can find religion tiresome and offensive (Isaiah 1:11-14). He isn't impressed by performances or outward appearances. He is far more interested in what is in our hearts. This was the problem with the Scribes and the Pharisees. Their words were impressive but their hearts were empty, and they were only interested in traditions taught by men (Matthew 15:8-9). Religion that God approves of isn't about being dressed in fine robes and performing meaningless rituals; it's about serving the needy out of a love for God and for those around us (James 1:27).

Nicodemus was intrigued by Jesus' talk about being born again and asked, "How can this be?"

Jesus didn't say much more to Nicodemus. There was no point in trying to explain how such heavenly things worked while people were still confused about how *earthly* things worked. Instead, Jesus gave Nicodemus a promise. Jesus claimed that he was the only person to have come to earth from Heaven, and so Nicodemus would have to trust that what he said was true.

The world is full of people who think that they know all about heaven. Everyone seems to be an expert and has their opinion on how to get there, what it will be like and whether or not we'll have wings. But how can anyone know? Jesus' claim is unique. He is the only person who came here from Heaven. We can trust what he says.

It was now late at night, but before leaving, Jesus said that he must be crucified so that everyone who believes in him may have eternal life. But what does that have to do with Nicodemus and religion?

Jesus is answering Nicodemus' question about how he could be born again. Religion and morals cannot give you a fresh start and a new identity, but through Jesus' death on the cross we can be forgiven for all the wrong things we have done and start over again. It is not about us trying to please God, but about us accepting that Jesus did everything to restore our relationship with God when he made his sacrifice on the cross.

Other than this conversation in John Chapter Three, Nicodemus is little more than a footnote in the Bible. His name is mentioned in passing on two further occasions, but both occasions show that a profound change had happened in Nicodemus. In John Chapter Seven he is seen leaping to the defence of Jesus in front of the Chief Priests and Pharisees. His former cowardice in front of his religious peers has gone, and he boldly stands up for Jesus when those around him are trying to find an excuse to arrest him.

The final time we see Nicodemus is at the foot of the cross (John 19:39), after Jesus has died. He has removed Jesus' bloodied corpse from the wooden scaffold and is embalming the body prior to laying it in the tomb. Jesus had been lifted up at the end of his life, and Nicodemus had been there to look up at him. One life had ended, but another had just begun. Nicodemus had been born again.

Just like the story of the rich young man, the story of Nicodemus leaves each of us with a decision to make. Will you be renewed, regenerated and receive a new identity? Will you put your trust in religion and try to please God that way, or will you allow Jesus to do it for you? Will you let the old you go to the grave with Jesus and allow a new life to begin with Jesus at the centre? Will you be born again?

SATISFACTION

∞

Jesus and the Bad Samaritan
John 4:4-42

As we continue our journey through the gospels it is just a short trip down the road into John Chapter Four. The location is Samaria. It's a run down, dilapidated destination, and many of us would rather alight at a leafy suburb further along the way. We have no choice, though. Jesus is stopping here, so we must follow. You see, he doesn't show partiality. He doesn't just want to meet with the more respectable characters that we've encountered in chapters one and two. In fact, as we get to know more about Jesus, we'll realise that this is where he spends a lot of his time. Jesus seems to have a penchant for associating with "sinners", and doesn't seem to mind spending his spare time in the less salubrious parts of town. He's even seen in public socialising with tax collectors and prostitutes, something that really annoyed the Scribes and the Pharisees (Mark 2:16).

In the days of Jesus, the Holy Land was divided into three portions: Galilee to the north, Judea to the south and Samaria in the middle. The origins of Samaria date back to the times when the Babylonians conquered the southern kingdom of Judah. The Babylonians took almost every person into captivity in Babylon but left behind a filthy remnant of undesirable citizens. Gradually other people groups moved into the void left by the Babylonian invasion, intermarried with the aforementioned undesirables and the "Samaritans" were formed. By the time Jesus came onto the scene the Samaritans were a melting pot of different races and religions. There was an element of Judaism left in them from the initial remnant that clung onto the teachings of the Old Testament, but this had been watered down and diluted with all sorts of pagan rituals and foreign gods. The "pure" Jews referred to the Samaritans as mongrels, guilty of desecrating their religious and cultural heritage. Emotions ran high between Jews and Samaritans, which could often overspill into violence and muggings. As a consequence, any ordinary Jew would circumnavigate Samaria on their way to Galilee for fear of reprisals or becoming unclean by association; but as we're beginning to see, Jesus was no ordinary Jew. Tired from the journey, Jesus sat down at a well whilst his disciples went into the nearby town to find some food. A Samaritan woman came to draw water from the well, and Jesus went to work.

The conversation began simply enough. Jesus asked the woman for a drink. For us that may seem like an entirely reasonable thing to do, but given the cultural context Jesus was actually being very controversial. According to first century Jewish customs men didn't talk to women, Jews didn't talk to Samaritans and – most of all – you didn't share a drinking vessel with a woman with like *that*.

You see, this woman wasn't simply a Samaritan; she was the worst of all Samaritans. As the conversation unfolded, it turned out that this woman was the talk of the town after a string of failed marriages and sordid affairs. The Samaritan woman was thrown by Jesus' apparent ignorance of the etiquette of the day, and asked him why someone like him would want to share a drink with someone like her. Jesus replied that if she knew who she was talking to then the roles would be reversed and she would have asked him for a drink instead. He went on to say that he would have provided her with something far better than warm water from a dusty well in Sychar. He would have given her Living Water.

The woman rose to the bait. What is this "Living Water"? Where do you get it from?

Jesus answered, "Everyone who drinks this water will be thirsty again, but whoever drinks the water I give him will never thirst. Indeed, the water I give him will become in him a spring of water welling up to eternal life." (verses 13 and 14). The woman was transfixed by the words falling from Jesus' lips. Eager to know more, she asked him for this water that would satisfy her thirst forever.

At this point, though, the conversation took a sharp and apparently random turn. Instead of telling the woman where she could get this water, Jesus asked the woman to bring along her husband. The woman replied with a coy half-truth. "I have no husband." Jesus, aware of her nefarious lifestyle, responded by saying that she was quite right in saying that she didn't have a husband. The truth was that she had had five previous husbands and that she wasn't married to the man she was currently living with.

Jesus was trying to show the woman how empty her life had become. She wasn't just thirsty for water, but was thirsty for fulfilment. She was lonely, and her life had no meaning or direction. She had tried to fill the emptiness with cheap relationships and it hadn't worked.

In 1961 scientists Lois and Theodore Zucker found that some rats had a genetic propensity towards obesity[2]. These rats were found to have faulty leptin receptors (leptin is a hormone which tells the brain that the body has had enough to eat). A group of rats were bred as a genetic model of obesity. Without the leptin receptors to tell the

---

[2] Zucker, L. M. and Zucker, T.F. (1961). *Fatty, a new mutation in the rat.* Journal of Heredity, 52:275-278

brain that the rat was full, the rats ate constantly, permanently locked in a world of hunger. As long as the rats were presented with food they would keep eating and never be satisfied until one day they died of heart failure.

When we fell out of our relationship with God we were left with a longing to be satisfied. Whether we know it or not, we all crave God. Deep down we're all suffering from the same affliction; an insatiable desire to be accepted, fulfilled and satisfied. We're a generation of consumers. The world tells us that life is all about how much you can get and how soon we can get it. Just like the Zucker rats, whatever we have isn't enough, and a hole remains that we know needs filling. Just a slightly bigger house, just a bit more money, and just a bit more stuff and then we'll be happy. Or so we are told. But what is there in this world that can truly satisfy us?

Once again I'm transported back to Narnia. This time I'm stood with Jill at the top of Aslan's Mountain at the beginning of *The Silver Chair*[3]. Jill is dying of thirst and is standing just a few feet away from a stream. However, between her and the stream stands the Great Lion. Aslan informs her that despite her worst fears, unless she comes to him and drinks his water then she will die of thirst. Jill is still not convinced, and asks if there is another stream

---

[3] *The Silver Chair*, C.S. Lewis, HarperCollins (1953)

which she can go to, but Aslan says no – there isn't any other stream. Eventually, Jill plucks up the courage and kneels down at Aslan's feet to drink, and the water is incredible – refreshing in a way that makes Jill feel instantly satisfied. She doesn't have to drink very much of it, and her thirst is gone.

The Bible tells us that it is only God who can truly satisfy us (Isaiah 55:1-2). There isn't any other stream. When we come to meet with God, something resonates in our hearts that tells us that we have always been missing Him. God wants you to stop chasing after things that won't make you happy and to find true fulfilment by being in a relationship with him. We can try to fill the empty space with sex, money, fast cars and alcohol, but at the end of the day it is only a relationship with God that can end the thirst we have for contentment. Jesus came to fill our emptiness. Jesus doesn't offer us something that will quench our thirst for a few short hours, but something that will make us completely clean and completely satisfied. Forever.

Following Jesus is about more than just qualifying for Heaven. It's about the here and now. Jesus came so that your life could be transformed from the inside out. He wants to change the direction of your life. He wants to show you a new path to walk that will lead to life in all its fullness (John 10:10). He wants to set us free from the damaging things in our life, so that our marriages, work and relationships can be more fulfilling than we ever imagined possible. He came so that we could learn the true meaning of enjoyment.

This short meeting with Jesus changed the Samaritan Woman. She was no longer thirsty and she left her water jar lying on the ground and ran off to town to tell everyone about the man she had just met at the well. Many people, just like the woman, came to believe in Jesus, and received the life-giving water he was offering. The local people were so taken with Jesus that they asked him to stay a while longer, which he did. What began as a murky, seedy narrative ended with the first revival recorded in the gospels. People's lives are changed as torrents of living water flow through the town. And where did this happen? In Sychar, in the heart of Samaria, the last place on earth that people thought would deserve a visit from God on earth.

The story of the Bad Samaritan isn't just about God wanting to make us happy, though. Above all else it's a story that tells us how God feels about us. It tells us that whatever you have done God won't give up on you because He has good things planned for your future (Jeremiah 29:11). There's nothing in your past that will exclude you from coming to meet with God. God sent Jesus to meet us where we are at the moment. He's not waiting for you to be perfect. He's not waiting for you to be more respectable. He knows you and all your faults already and He wants to give you a second chance.

When the world tells us we're a lost cause, Jesus says there is still hope. His love for us is far reaching and in Sychar we've seen it stretch down into the most rejected parts of society and claim the most unlikely of candidates for Heaven. He wants to have you back in his family, wherever you have been and whatever you have done. You are his treasure, and God would give everything He has to get you back. In the next chapter we will see the lengths he is prepared to go to in order to give you that chance.

FORGIVENESS

∞

Jesus and the Penitent Thief
Luke 23:39-47

As we climb the hill to Calvary, where Jesus died, we are met with a horrifying scene. Instead of finding Jesus sat talking with friends, teaching his disciples or taking a boat trip on the Sea of Galilee, we find him hung between two common thieves, nailed to a wooden cross, the device of torture and execution devised by the Persians and perfected by the Romans. The Romans crucified literally thousands of people, and as the centurions arrived for work that morning they little suspected that today would be different to any other day. However, as we are about to see, the crucifixion of Jesus of Nazareth that afternoon was to be the most significant event in human history.

Jesus' crucifixion is even more surprising when we consider the events of a week previously. Just a few days earlier Jesus had ridden into Jerusalem on the back of a borrowed colt (Mark 11:7). The crowds had come out to meet him, waved palm branches (a symbol of victory and celebration) and praised God: Israel's long-awaited King had arrived. The two scenes couldn't be more different. What had happened during that week to transform Jesus from a worshipped King into a crucified criminal?

When we are looking for someone to blame for Jesus' death there are no shortage of culprits. We can blame the religious leaders for their scheming and skulduggery. We can blame Judas for betraying Jesus in exchange for thirty pieces of silver (Matthew 26:15). We can blame Pilate or Herod for not having the guts to release Jesus when they found no fault in him (Luke 23:14-15). We can blame the crowd for shouting "Crucify him!", or the Roman soldiers for nailing him to a cross. Or we can blame ourselves for the sin which took him there, and take collective responsibility for his brutal death.

All of these reasons have an element of truth to them, but they don't get to the heart of the matter and explain why Jesus was really crucified all those years ago. Jesus died because it was all part of God's plan for the world. Before the creation of the world God knew that mankind would go astray. God also knew that in order to get us back, the ultimate price would have to be paid. When we look at the story of the first Easter it is important to remember that the only person who really knew what was going on was Jesus. It was part of the plan. It was the reason he came to earth in the first place. Jesus didn't fall victim to social, political or religious forces outside of his control. No one took his life from him, he gave it away voluntarily (John 10:18). Jesus went to the cross as an act of obedience. Jesus died because God asked him to (Isaiah 53:10).

And so it was that Jesus was led away to be crucified between two thieves, one on the left of him, and one on the right. All four gospel accounts record the presence of the two criminals crucified on either side of Jesus, but it is only Luke who records the fascinating conversation that took place between these three men as they died.

Whilst Jesus hung on the cross the watching crowd sneered and hurled insults at him, saying, "He saved others; let him save himself if he is the Christ of God, the Chosen One." One of the criminals joined with the crowd and railed against Jesus, asking him to save himself and his fellow victims from their impending fate, but the other criminal rebuked him. "Don't you fear God," he said, "since you are under the same sentence? We are punished justly, for we are getting what our deeds deserve. But this man has done nothing wrong." Then he said, "Jesus, remember me when you come into your kingdom." This man's shameful existence and depraved lifestyle had earned him the death sentence, and yet he resorted to one final throw of the dice to try and avoid what his life had deserved. Would Jesus accept a deathbed conversion from a career criminal? Would his forgiveness stretch that far?

Forgiveness is a controversial subject. We recognise that making mistakes is all part of being human, but who can be forgiven – and under what circumstances? We might feel able to turn a blind eye to some minor indiscretions, but for more serious crimes we deem that an apology or even punishment is necessary. We may even go so far as to say that the most serious offences are unforgiveable. And if ever we are in any doubt about who is worthy of forgiveness then the media are always willing to lend a helping hand with emotive headlines telling us how we should feel about certain people. When it comes to forgiveness, where do we draw the line? More to the point, where does God draw the line?

The Bible tells us that God has a standard and his standard is perfection. The Bible also tells us that we have all fallen short of that target (Romans 3:23). God isn't interested in near misses. God wants perfection from us, but none of us have achieved it. To make matters worse, the price for failure isn't just an apology or reparations. The price of failure is separation from God. The biggest problem that any one of us will ever face isn't financial, or related to our health and wellbeing. Our greatest problem is that we haven't lived up to God's standards. It's a problem that none of us can escape on our own – but the good news is that Jesus can offer us a solution.

During my time at university I scaled the literary heights of reading the unabridged version of Victor Hugo's Les Miserables. It is the story of Jean Valjean, his adopted daughter Cosette, and her revolutionary lover Marius, set against the backdrop of the French Revolution. After I ploughed through the 1600 pages the weighty tome now sits proudly on my bookcase, a testament to my patience, perseverance and abysmal time-management skills. In all honesty I'll probably never read it again, but I indulge myself on a regular basis by watching Rafael Yglesias's 1998 film adaptation starring Liam Neeson as Jean Valjean.

In the penultimate scene of the 1998 film version[4], Jean Valjean carries the wounded Marius through the Parisian sanitation network, back to Cosette. Cosette is overjoyed that her father and lover have escaped from the throes of the revolution. However, the chimera of happy families evaporates moments later with the appearance of a Gendarme in the doorway, pistol in hand. Cosette realises what has happened: Valjean knew the punishment that Marius deserved and agreed to take the punishment for him. He knew that the only way he could set his children free was by dying in their place. Before going to meet his fate the loving father embraces his child and utters the

---

[4] *Les Miserables* was produced in 1998 by Studio Eiv, and was directed by Raphael Iglesias

immortal words, "I've made an arrangement... I don't mind paying."

Jesus is God's solution to the problem of sin. Jesus succeeded where we failed. He was able to live the perfect life that God found acceptable. When Jesus went to the cross, he made an exchange, because when he died Jesus received the punishment that we deserved – separation from God. He took the judgement for our failure so that we wouldn't have to. He was punished by God so that we could have peace with God (Isaiah 53:5). The Penitent Thief trusted in Jesus, and Jesus answered him, "I tell you the truth, today you will be with me in Paradise".

Before their meeting on Calvary, the two criminals either side of Jesus had presumably led similar lives. There is no moral distinction that can be drawn between these two men, but when they met Jesus, one responded with humility while the other responded with mockery. The key to forgiveness – the key to Heaven – isn't in what we've done or how the world sees us, it is in how we respond to the offer Jesus is making. In meeting Jesus face to face, the Penitent Thief not only learned who Jesus was, he also learned a lot about himself. He understood that he had done things wrong and that he deserved to the judgement he was facing. Despite his situation, though, the Penitent Thief was not despondent. The answer to all of his problems was hanging on an identical scaffold just a few feet away. There was no cleverly constructed façade, no attempt to impress Jesus, and no scheme to avoid punishment. He merely admitted his shortcomings and asked for forgiveness. God's offer to us is that because of Jesus we can do the same.

Sooner or later, we will all realise that the story of the two criminals on either side of the cross is actually all about us and the choice we have to make. All of us have fallen short of God's standard, but the cross of Jesus is where God's love meets our sin. We deserve the same judgement that the two thieves faced, but God loved the world so much that he sent Jesus so that if we believe in him we won't perish but instead receive everlasting life (John 3:16).

The human condition is one of utter desperation. Each of us has turned to his own way and fallen short of God's perfect standard, but Jesus came to earth to take our punishment. We owe a debt that we cannot possibly repay. The good news – the gospel – is that through Jesus the debt can be cancelled, leaving us free to enjoy all the good things of Heaven. We all have a choice to make. Will we be like the first criminal and reject Jesus' offer, or will we allow him to pay the price for our sins?

It's OK. He's made an arrangement. He doesn't mind paying.

SUFFERING

∞

Jesus and Cleopas
Luke 24:13-35

On 22 November 1963, President John F. Kennedy was being driven through Dallas during a political trip to Texas. At the age of only 46, he was the second youngest President of the United States of America. At 12:30pm, two gun shots rang out. The first one hit him in the back, and the second hit him in the back of the head, killing the young President instantly. He was rushed to Parkland Hospital for emergency medical treatment but was pronounced dead at 1:00 pm.

A wave of public grief followed, and during the next three years a staggering sixteen million people attended John F. Kennedy's grave. But for his family, the assassination of President Kennedy was just another incident in a long line of tragedies. Their misfortunes have been well documented. During the twentieth century, the Kennedy family were subjected to more than their fair share of suffering – experiencing a failed lobotomy, stillborn children, numerous fatal aeroplane and car crashes, two assassinations and a fatal skiing accident.

One of the biggest objections people have to existence of God is the presence of suffering in the world. In the global village we now live in, pain and suffering have never been closer to home. Twenty-four hour news programmes give a constant reminder that there is something fundamentally wrong with the world, and images of catastrophe are never more than a red button away. What's more, pain is no respecter of position or reputation. It is an unavoidable part of life and no one is immune, even the most powerful person in the world. The problem of pain is that, one way or another, it will always find a way to our door. Whatever our background, whatever our worldview, and whatever our decisions in life, we know that one day illness, bereavement or loss will come to visit us. Whichever way we look we see injustice, and God just turns a blind eye. What is His response to this cosmic tragedy? Where is God when it hurts?

The presence of suffering in our world poses probing questions to people of all faiths and none. Where did suffering come from? Does it mean that God doesn't exist? If not, then is He a helpless spectator to our plight? Does He care about us?

The Bible teaches that God made a perfect, harmonious and good creation (Genesis 1:31). When He had finished creating the world and the surrounding universe, God crowned His creation by placing mankind on the earth. However, God also gave us the freedom to make our own choices. When mankind first made a choice to go our own way rather than God's way this wonderful creation was thrown into disarray (Romans 8:21-22). The pain and suffering with which we are all too familiar were never intended to be part of God's original plan for His creation. God made a perfect creation for us to live in, and we have ruined it by thinking that we knew best. And we live with the consequences. We are broken people living in a broken world, and suffering is inevitable.

But is that the end of the story? Do we just have to tolerate the pain and suffering for 75 years before slipping into an endless sleep? Or is there something else we haven't seen? Does God have a plan?

On the Sunday afternoon following Jesus' crucifixion, two of Jesus' followers were making the seven-mile trip home from Jerusalem to Emmaus. The Bible identifies one of these travellers as Cleopas, and the assumption is often made that his companion was his wife. Like most other people in and around Jerusalem at the time, there was only one topic in their conversation; the strange events over the Passover feast and the claims of the women that Jesus had risen from the dead. Unbeknownst to them, as they walked and talked Jesus himself came up and walked along with them. The Bible tells us that "they were kept from recognising him", and that Jesus joined their conversation by asking the question, "What are you discussing together as you walk along?"

From the outside Cleopas looked "downcast", but his reply to Jesus revealed more of how he was feeling beneath the surface. Cleopas was disappointed. Cleopas and his wife had followed Jesus closely for several years. They had seen him operate at close quarters, healing the sick and cleansing lepers, and they had made the decision to dedicate their lives to him. And why? They hoped that he was the one who was going to be the Messiah, the promised King – they believed he would usher in a glorious new age for Israel. They had pinned their hopes on Jesus restoring a kingdom and driving out the occupying power of Rome. After many a false dawn, Jesus of Nazareth finally seemed to be the person everyone had been waiting for. He ticked all the boxes, fulfilled all the prophecies and then...died.

Cleopas wasn't just disappointed with Jesus though. Jesus' prediction of his own death and resurrection, along with the message of the angels and the empty tomb had left Cleopas confused.. In the depths of sorrow and disappointment, Cleopas and his wife had been trying to put together the few pieces of the puzzle that they had at their disposal. In addition to hoping that Jesus would redeem Israel, Cleopas also noted that this was the third day since Jesus had been crucified. Yet still they didn't understand, and they continued on in their quest to discover exactly what had happened on Good Friday, and whether the events of that morning were the fulfilment of prophecy or just another unanswered question, just another disappointment.

Yes, Cleopas was disappointed with Jesus. He had placed his trust in him and Jesus had let him down badly. If we are honest with ourselves, there have been times when we have felt the same way too. Famines strike, droughts parch the land, tsunamis hit coastlines and the good die young. We look at the evidence and come to the only logical conclusion: that God either isn't there, or doesn't care. At some point in our lives we have all had to walk a mile in Cleopas' shoes. It is at times like this that we turn to God and ask "Why?" God created this world, and supposedly He is in charge. Why can't He sort out this mess we're all in? What is the plan?

Jesus' response was to give Cleopas the bigger picture. Using age-old Biblical stories as his text, Jesus took Cleopas out of the immediacy of his situation and explained how the events of that weekend were all part of God's bigger plan, a plan so vast that Cleopas hadn't been able to understand it whilst in the midst of his suffering.

As they approached their destination, Jesus acted as if he were going further. But they urged him strongly, "Stay with us, for it is nearly evening; the day is almost over." Jesus agreed, and went in to stay with them. When he was at the table with them, he took the bread, gave thanks, broke it and began to give it to them. At that moment something profound happened within Cleopas and his companion; their eyes were opened and they recognised Jesus – but he disappeared from their sight.

God's plan is to have sent Jesus to die in our place so that we could have a ticket out of the pain and suffering. He came to reverse the consequences of our sin. He came to heal the brokenness that we see in ourselves and in the world around us. He wants to take broken people and make them new. What is more, He wants to take us out of this broken creation and place us in a new creation, where things will be as they were always meant to be. However difficult life has been on earth, the troubles we face here are only light and momentary compared with all the good things that God has in store for us in Heaven (Romans 8:18). There will be no more pain, no more crying, no more illness and no more death (Revelation 21:4). He loves us so much that he would do anything to give us that opportunity, even sending His only Son to die in our place. He became broken so that we no longer need to be.

Having Heaven to look forward to is one thing, but what about now? It sounds good to know that one day the pain will come to an end, but is that all that Jesus can offer us –

that if we grin and bear it until we die, then hopefully there will be something better over the horizon?

During the American Revolution three soldiers were struggling to build a rampart out of logs. Their Corporal stood by, idly barking out orders and instructions. Just then a man in civilian clothes approached on a horse. He asked the Corporal why he would not help the soldiers in their struggles, but the reply came back that he was a Corporal, and such tasks were beneath him. On hearing this, the man jumped off his horse and helped the three soldiers to finish their task. He then turned to the Corporal, unbuttoned his coat to reveal a military uniform, and told him that if ever his men were struggling with a task that he considered beneath him, then the Corporal should ask him for help. With that, George Washington, Commander-in-Chief of the American army, remounted his horse and rode on, one day to become the first President of the United States of America.

There have been many leaders who have shown tactical acumen, military prowess and economic astuteness, but what sets George Washington apart as one of the great leaders of his, or any, generation was his ability to remain humble despite his lofty status. He was a leader who was always willing to get off his horse, roll up his sleeves and get his hands dirty if he saw someone in need. George Washington was able to be sympathetic to the struggles of his people because he was willing to share in their situation.

God could have left the human race stranded forever in the mess that it had made, but He loves us too much to do that. God didn't leave us here on our own, but came to live with us as Jesus. He saw the problems we were facing and came to experience them too. Jesus wore our clothes and walked in our shoes for thirty-three years. Jesus left the comfort and security of Heaven in order to become acquainted with the pain and the sorrow that we suffer on a daily basis.

Jesus doesn't just want to give us a hope for the future; he wants to give us help for today. He is sympathetic to our needs because he's felt the same pain that we feel (Hebrews 4:14-18). He knows what it's like to be born into abject poverty and to spend his childhood as a refugee. He knows what it's like to shed tears at the death of a close friend. He knows what it's like to be laughed at, mocked, spat upon, whipped and beaten. He knows what it's like to be deserted by friends and family at his time of greatest need. He knows what it's like to have his Father turn his back on him, and to be punished for something he didn't do. He knows what it's like to be an innocent victim and die a brutal death. When we take our problems to Jesus we don't take them to a distant despot who doesn't know what it's like to feel pain, but to sympathetic Saviour who knows exactly how we're feeling.

Jesus changes the way we look at suffering. The pain won't go away today, but our perspective can change. We will still grieve at times, but not without hope (1 Thessalonians 4:13). He helps us to see that despite all the pain and suffering around us there is a much bigger plan being worked out. With him in our lives, pain is no longer pointless and futile but tells us that there is something wrong with the world. Walking with Jesus tells us that he came to fix the problem and that one day we can be free from all the pain, disappointment and confusion. Walking with Jesus is walking with a friend who has been there before and knows how we're feeling. While we are in this world we will all feel pain, but God sent Jesus to accompany us through every scene of life, and at the end of the road He will wipe away every tear from our eyes.

Where is God when it hurts? He's walking right beside us, every step of the way.

DOUBT

∞

Jesus and Thomas
John 20:19-31

On the same day that Jesus had appeared to Cleopas and his companion on the road to Emmaus, he also appeared to some of the other disciples, in Jerusalem later that evening. The disciples had been together, hidden in a closed room with the doors locked for fear of the religious powers that be. They had seen Jesus' horrific demise and they were worried that they might be next.

The locked doors were no barrier to Jesus, though. He came and stood among them and said, "Peace be with you!" After he said this, he showed them his hands and side. The disciples were overjoyed. Maybe the stories they had heard from the women who found the empty tomb were true after all. They had seen him, and they began to believe.

However, not all of the disciples were present when Jesus appeared. Thomas had not been there, and when the other disciples told him that they had also seen Jesus, his response was cynical. "Unless I see the nail marks in his hands and put my finger where the nails were, and put my hand into his side, I will not believe it".

Thomas wasn't someone who could be easily fooled. He wasn't going to be conned by a group of wishful thinkers clinging on to a dying dream. You had to be rational about these things. Seeing was believing, and anything less wouldn't suffice.

The spirit of Thomas is alive and well today. We live in an age of scepticism. The world tells us that anything which can't be proved by cold hard facts and corroborating evidence is to be discarded. Rational thought is king, and any belief system that can't be proved empirically must be dismissed as delusional at best and dangerous at worst. Faith is obsolete, a relic of a fallen empire that reigned victorious in an age when men had small minds and high hopes. Proponents of non-scientific belief systems are viewed with suspicion and are derided in the media as being infantile and superstitious. Faith is dead, and intelligence has killed it.

Science is a wonderful thing. It has brought so many good things to the human race. It has increased our knowledge of the world we live in, and the amazing universe of which we are only a miniscule part. Medical advancements have found cures for diseases that previously claimed thousands of lives. Our standard of living has increased beyond measure, and no one deserves more credit than the men and women in white coats who dedicate their lives to improving our existence. We owe them a huge debt of gratitude.

There are questions, however, that science has never been able to answer, and never will be. We fall into the trap of assuming that we have the capacity to know and understand everything. But what if there are some things which are forever beyond our comprehension? The advancements of science will always be limited by the boundaries of the human mind. The danger of adopting an exclusively scientific approach to life is that each passing generation believes itself to be the Enlightened Ones, believing that they have finally cracked the code of life and the universe. Then the research of subsequent generations inevitably reveals the mistakes of the past. We need to accept that we're not always the experts. We don't know everything. We can't know everything.

Charles F. Kettering was one of the great innovative minds of the twentieth century. Kettering became the vice president of the General Motors Research Corporation in 1920, and remained in that post until 1947. He was an engineer by trade, but as an inventor he held 186 patents. Amongst his achievements are the invention of the electrical starting motor and leaded gasoline, as well as harnessing the technology to mass-produce painted vehicles, making the world's first aerial missile, and developing a primitive air-conditioning system.

The secret to Kettering's success wasn't just that he had a great mind, though. Kettering was able to do things that were previously thought impossible because he didn't rely on existing knowledge to come up with new solutions. During his time as Head of Research at General Motors, if he faced a problem that required new technology he would call an amnesty on all mathematical equipment. He would leave a table outside his office, where his research team would deposit their slide rules and set squares. He knew that if his engineers relied upon maths alone to solve a problem then they would only find new ways of failing. Taking their equipment away from them made them think in different ways and look at things from a different perspective.

If we want to meet with God then we need to start to think in new ways. Ever since the start of its existence, the human race has tried to find a way back to God. Moralists try to find God with rules, religious people try to find God with rituals, and scientists try to find God with reasoning. All three approaches are doomed to failure. They don't find God – and so we come to the conclusion that He isn't there. However, the Bible tells us that God's ways are above our ways (Isaiah 55:8-9). He is beyond our comprehension. We can't work Him out like a maths problem. For all its benefits, science can't find God.

Christianity accepts that there is a gap between God and man which we cannot cross. The only reason we can meet God is that He has already come to meet us first. In sending Jesus into the world, God revealed himself to us; and this revelation can succeed where rules, rituals and reasoning have all failed. When Jesus came to earth he crossed a divide that we could never traverse on our own. Because of Jesus, God became tangible. Because of Jesus, God is close enough to touch.

A week later the disciples were all together in the house again. Once again the doors were locked, but this time Thomas was with them. Just like a week before, Jesus came and stood amongst them and said, "Peace be with you!" Then he turned to Thomas and said, "Put your fingers here; see my hands. Reach out your hand and put it into my side. Stop doubting and believe." Thomas did stop doubting and believed. Meeting Jesus put his doubting mind at rest, and he said to Jesus, "My Lord and my God!"

During his time on earth, people often came to Jesus and asked him for a miracle (Matthew 16:4). They were thirsty for evidence. They had heard good things about Jesus, but it all sounded too good to be true. They wanted more from Jesus. Just one more sign and perhaps they could believe.

They didn't want to base their faith on hearsay; they wanted to see something impressive for themselves.

People today are just the same. The idea of Jesus sounds a very inviting one, but how can we be sure? We feel that God owes us something. We want God to put on a performance for us. We feel instinctively that if He is really there, then he should prove himself. We want to see something spectacular. If God really wants our affections, then he should do something about it and raise His head above the parapet every now and then. Not something vague or ambiguous, but something dramatic and conclusive which puts His existence and His love for us beyond all reasonable doubt.

If we want to find evidence for God, we need to start looking in the right place. When God sent Jesus into the world He did something dramatic and conclusive. The sign for Jesus' generation is the same as the sign for our generation: that God loved the world so much that He sent His own Son here on a rescue mission. The evidence for God isn't in finding new signs, but trusting in the sign that He has already sent. Jesus came so that we would have something real, something physical, to base our faith on. He's not an apparition. He's not an abstract concept. He was a real life person walking amongst us. When Thomas met Jesus he knew beyond all reasonable doubt that this man really was who he claimed to be.

Jesus wants us all to have an experience like the one that Thomas had. Our stoic attitudes and closed minds have made having faith difficult, but if we are willing to trust in him then God has promised to give us the evidence that each of us needs.

God isn't hiding from you. If we want to see evidence for God then all we need to do is look around us. He's made himself self-evident by the wonderful creation He has placed us in (Romans 1:19). He's promised that if we call on Him then he will hear us. He's promised that if we seek Him with all our heart we will find Him, and that when we find Him we will be welcomed into His family (Jeremiah 29:12-13).

When Jesus came to earth he left an indelible mark on the human race. His life was a demonstration of what God is like, and in dying he showed us how much God loves us. God isn't distant. Jesus wants us to accept his invitation of a relationship with him so that we can discover what God is like for ourselves. Christianity isn't just a worldview to be discussed, it's a relationship to be experienced. When we begin to experience that relationship, all our questions, doubts and fears melt away. He doesn't want us to remain impartial spectators. He wants us to be involved. He wants to give us something to base our faith on. He wants us to reach out and touch him, to feel him, and to know with all certainty that he's there and that he loves us.

God is calling an amnesty on the way we used to think. He wants us to open our hearts and our minds to new ideas. He wants you to give faith a chance so that you can be sure about the things you hope for and certain about the things you can't see. The evidence for God isn't found in a laboratory, it's displayed in the amazing creation that He's placed us in. More than that, it's in the reality of experiencing a relationship with Jesus for ourselves. Can you dare to be different? Can you stop doubting? Can you believe?

FAILURE

∞

Jesus and Simon Peter
John 17-21

As we near the end of our journey through the stories of Jesus there is one person who has so far been notable by his absence. Of all the people who Jesus met in the Bible, no one has more dialogue recorded than Simon Peter. Peter was the disciple to speak up first whenever a question needed answering, or an opinion was sought. People have always had a special affection for Peter. He is someone we can easily relate to, because he had so many endearing qualities. He was bold, courageous and enthusiastic. He was a hero, the kind of person you would want next to you when the going got tough. However, Peter was a flawed hero and there were times when his self-confidence was misplaced, sometimes with tragic consequences.

The Bible isn't sentimental in its recollections. Each character we meet is exposed and vulnerable, and the accounts we read are transparent and honest. We see the good and bad in each person, and the same is true for Peter.

At times we find a great example to follow, but at other times his life is a cautionary tale from which we can learn valuable lessons. He had good days and he had bad days. As he walked through life he experienced exhilarating highs and soul-destroying lows. He tasted the sweetness of success and the bitterness of failure in equal measure. He was someone just like us.

The Bible includes many stories involving Peter, some more famous than others. However, by far the most well-known – and most tragic – story occurred just before Jesus was crucified. During the Last Supper Jesus had told his disciples that he would have to go away, and that where he was going they would not be able to follow. Peter protested, "Lord, why can't I follow you now? I will lay down my life for you." Jesus answered, "Will you really lay down your life for me? I tell you the truth, before the cock crows you will disown me three times."

The events that unfolded over the next few hours showed that Jesus' words were true. After going to pray in the Garden of Gethsemane, Jesus was betrayed by Judas Iscariot, one of the original twelve disciples, who led a detachment of soldiers and religious leaders to arrest Jesus. Jesus was taken away to be tried, and Peter followed at a distance. When they arrived at the high priest's courtyard the girl guarding the door recognised Peter and asked, "Aren't you one of the disciples?" He replied "I am not," and the girl allowed him entry into the courtyard. It was a cold night, and Peter went to join the servants and officials who were warming themselves by the fire.

Whilst he was stood warming himself one of the servants asked him again if he was one of the disciples and for a second time Peter said no. Finally, one of the high priest's servants challenged him. "Didn't I see you with Jesus in the Garden of Gethsemane?" Just as Jesus had predicted, Peter denied knowing him for a third time, angrily protesting "I don't know the man!" Just as he was speaking the cock crowed. Jesus turned and looked at Peter, and he remembered the words Jesus had spoken to him just a few hours earlier.

Peter had tasted failure before, but nothing on this scale. He knew what it was like to get it all wrong and look stupid in front of his friends, but this time things were much more serious. He was a proud man who enjoyed his own courage, valour and loyalty, but he had let himself down badly. His famed bravery had left him. He had deserted the person he called Lord – the person who he had promised to follow to the end only a few hours earlier – during his hour of greatest need.. Peter was devastated. There was no way back from something like this. He went outside and wept bitterly. He was a failure, and he knew it. It was the end of the road, and Jesus was led away to be crucified.

After appearing to Thomas and the other disciples after his resurrection, Jesus appeared to his disciples another time, this time at the Sea of Galilee. The disciples had returned to Galilee and Peter, as ever the spokesman for the group, had decided to go fishing. Several of the other disciples decided to go with him, but that night they caught nothing.

Early the next morning Jesus stood on the shore, but the disciples did not realise that it was him. He called out to them, "Friends, haven't you caught any fish?" "No," they answered. Jesus replied, "Throw your net on the right side of the boat and you will find some." When they did, they were unable to haul the net in because of the large number of fish. The disciples realised that it must be Jesus, and returned to shore as fast as they could. Peter couldn't wait, and jumped off the boat to swim to shore. When they landed they found Jesus cooking breakfast for them on some burning coals.

The memory of Peter's denial lingered in the air. When they had finished eating, Jesus took Peter for a walk along the beach. We can only imagine what must have been going through Peter's mind as Jesus took him away privately. No doubt he would have been overcome with guilt, shame and embarrassment. What had started as a wonderful relationship had been ruined by Peter's cowardice. There were no secrets. Jesus knew everything. What would Jesus say to someone who had let him down so badly, who had failed so spectacularly?

Instead of piling on the misery, condemning him and telling him that his services would no longer be required, Jesus had a different message for Peter. He had a question that he wanted to ask him. He asked him it three times. He wanted to know if Peter still loved him. When Peter replied that he did Jesus gave him a job to do. In a few short days Jesus would be leaving this world behind and he needed someone to look after the other believers. He wanted someone to lead them. He wanted someone he could rely on. He wanted someone who was bold, courageous and enthusiastic. He wanted someone who had learned to trust in God's strength, not his own. He wanted Peter.

At times we have all felt like Peter. We let ourselves down. We start with good intentions and show a lot of potential, but somewhere along the way it all goes horribly wrong. Somehow we don't live up to our parents' expectations, or fail to be the reliable friend that we would like to think we are. We don't live up to our own hype. The same is true in our relationship with God. We make commitments and promises from honourable motives but one day we come across our own fallibility. We're not quite as strong as we thought we were, and inevitably we make a mess of things. It's easy to give up, but Jesus tells us that if we still love him then there is still hope.

One of the most memorable events of the 1992 Olympic Games in Barcelona was the men's 400 metre semi-final. The Great Britain sprinter Derek Redmond was in a rich vein of form. He had recorded the fastest time in the first round, and had gone on to win his quarter-final. His dad, Jim Redmond, stood watching in the crowd, and as the starting gun blasted there were high hopes that Derek Redmond would achieve his lifelong ambition and qualify for an Olympic final.

The race started well for Redmond, but with about 250 metres of the race remaining, disaster struck. Redmond's hamstring broke, and he crumpled in a heap on the track. His dreams were over and he was never to race in a major international event again. But what happened next has become part of Olympic folklore. Redmond got up and limped through the rest of the race. On the home straight he was joined by his father, who placed a loving arm around his son. Together they finished the race to a standing ovation of 70,000 spectators in the stadium and millions of viewers all over the globe. Derek Redmond had failed to reach the final but he had finished the race, and at the end of the day that was all that mattered to his proud father.

Jesus wants to tell us, like he told Peter, that he still has work for us to do, that he still wants us on his team. He wants to tell us that the race isn't over and that he has a plan for us if only we would get up and carry on.

It's easy to leave the race after a disappointment, but Jesus came to earth to pick us up, dust us down and help us over the finish line. He won't look at you as a lost cause, no matter how badly you've fallen. Jesus knows that we will all fall down along the way. He's not happy when we do, but it's never the end of the story. He wants you to know that if you still love him, you can be forgiven and restored. Each of us can have a place on his team and be given an important job to do in his Kingdom. Even if we give up on ourselves, Jesus won't give up on us. He wants you to finish the race because there's an amazing prize waiting for everyone who does.

Jesus has marked out a race for you. It's your race. No one else can run it for you. He knows that there will be times when you stumble, but he wants you run the race with perseverance. He'll be there to help you up every time you fall. He wants you to lay aside the things that are holding you back, the things that entangle you and trip you up along the way. He wants you to fix your eyes on him, so that you don't grow weary or lose heart. Jesus came to meet us so that we could be given a second chance, even when we let him down. He's here to help you finish the race so that he can give you your prize, the crown of life, eternity with him. It's why he came to meet us. It's what he created you for in the first place. It's your destiny, if you choose to accept it.

In Heaven there's a crown with your name on it. Go and get it. Get up and finish the race.

CONCLUSION

∞

Jesus and You
Matthew 16:13-20

"Taste and see that the Lord is good"
Psalm 34:8

When Jesus came to live amongst us, he voluntarily placed himself on trial. He took up his position in the dock and spent his whole life being questioned and cross-examined. He presented his evidence over thirty-three years and the eye witnesses have now delivered their statements.

That's not the end of the story, though. At the end of each trial, the jury is dismissed to review the evidence they have seen, and to come to a decision. The focus of attention has turned to us. We are the jury, and it's time for us to cast our vote. Do we believe that Jesus really was who he claimed to be?

People have always debated the validity of Jesus' claim to be the Son of God. What do we make of him? Was he someone who simply had delusions of grandeur, believing himself to be something he wasn't? Was he merely a gifted orator who swept people along in the religious fervour of the day, offering up profundities and pithy sayings on demand? Was he a real person at all, or do the stories just come from oral tradition and folklore? Or was he who he said he was: God living with us, sent on a mission to save us?

Even during his time on earth people had different ideas about who Jesus was. This led to a conversation between Jesus and his disciples. One day, as they were walking through Caesarea Philippi, Jesus turned to the disciples and said, "Who do people say that I am?" They replied, "Some say you are John the Baptist, others say Elijah, and yet others say you are Jeremiah or one of the prophets." Jesus didn't just want to know the opinions of others, though. He wanted to make his question personal. Probing deeper he asked, "But what about you? Who do you say I am?" (John 4:39-42).

Two thousand years of history have elapsed since that day, but Jesus' question remains the same. He wants to ask us all the same question. He doesn't want to ask his question in a group setting, by a show of hands, or in a secret ballot. He wants to ask each person individually. He wants to ask us face to face. He wants to know what your answer is, not anyone else's. If Jesus really is who he claimed to be, then his question to us is the most important question of all. It is a question that won't go away, and whether we like it or not, one day we too will have to give an answer.

People have spent centuries trying to answer the question of who Jesus is. We all have the same evidence at our disposal. We can read the same stories, listen to the same debates and study the same books, but somehow we can't agree on the same answer. Why is there so much diversity in our response to who Jesus was, despite the rich body of evidence at our fingertips? There must be something more than books, more than historical records, to help us find an answer. It was OK for the disciples, they had a real live person to go and speak with, but what about us?

I love books about history. My bookcase at home is full of dusty old books about events I never witnessed and people I never met. At the end of each biographical account there is a temptation to feel like an expert on whichever historical person you've been reading about. When you've read up in such detail about someone's life you often feel as if you've met them yourself, that you know them inside out, as if you've talked long into the night with them, discussing things in depth and learning what that person is really like.

The reality is altogether different, though. You don't get to know someone properly just by learning a series of facts about them. If you want to get to know someone, you need to spend time with them. It's not enough just to learn information about them from a book. If you want to go beyond the superficial, to learn what someone is really like, then you need to engage with them and enter into a relationship with them. The same is true with God. We shouldn't just take other people's stories for granted. Getting to know God isn't something we can learn from a book or be taught by others (Galatians 1:12). If we want to know God then we need to have a relationship with Him. We can't just rely on second-hand accounts. We need to test things out for ourselves.

After the Bad Samaritan had met with Jesus, she went away and enthusiastically told everyone who would listen about Jesus. Many of the Samaritans in that town came to believe in Jesus because of her story. They didn't just take her story for granted, though, they came and met Jesus for themselves. They said to the woman, "We no longer believe just because of what you said; now we have heard for ourselves, and we know that this man really is the Saviour of the world."

When Jesus left the earth and returned to Heaven, he didn't leave us on our own. He left us with a Helper (John 14:16). We call this Helper the Holy Spirit. Just as Jesus was God living *with* us, the Holy Spirit is God living *within* us. The Holy Spirit was a lasting gift from Jesus to us. Jesus told us that if ever we wanted the Holy Spirit then all we had to do was ask God for it. God is a generous Father who loves to give gifts to His children, and the Holy Spirit is a gift that He has promised to never withhold from us.

When Jesus was explaining to his disciples what the Holy Spirit was like, he told them that it would come to make its home in the heart of every believer and that it would continue Jesus' work in our lives (John 14:23). It would teach us and remind us of all the things that Jesus had said (John 14:26). It would guide us into the truth by speaking into our hearts the things which Jesus wanted to communicate to us (John 16:13). It was given to us to equip us to live for God, helping to transform us into people more and more like Jesus. Finally, it would enable us to know with certainty just who Jesus is (1 Corinthians 12:3), and to echo the answer that Simon Peter gave to Jesus' question as they walked through Caesarea Philippi: "You are the Messiah, the Son of the living God."

When Jesus came to live amongst us he came to speak with us, to answer our questions, and to give solutions to the problems we face. He came to show us what God is like. He came so that we could have a relationship with God, so that we could experience God rather than just knowing about Him. When it was time for him to leave us he gave us his gift of the Holy Spirit so that that relationship would never end, so that every person who has ever lived would have the opportunity to meet with God and to experience what He is really like. The gift of the Holy Spirit means that the lines of communication between us and God are never closed. The Holy Spirit means that the Bible is more than just a biography or a history book, it's the story of a relationship between us and our Creator, a relationship that we can participate in and experience for ourselves.

When Jesus came to earth he opened a dialogue with the human race. He left us all with a question and he's waiting for your answer. It's time to join the conversation.

Afterword

When John sat down to write his account of Jesus' life he had to be selective. He had done his homework and gathered hundreds of different stories about Jesus from the people who knew him best. If he had used each and every story he would have eventually filled dozens of large volumes. Instead, he set about selecting only a handful of stories. He only used the stories that he thought would most help his readers get to know Jesus for themselves (John 20:31; 21:25).

In some small way I've felt the same way as John did all those years ago. In a book this size it's only possible to scratch the surface. The gospels are full of stories about Jesus. In each story we find Jesus meeting someone different and sharing his message with them in new ways. He is a multi-faceted diamond, and from each angle we learn something new about him and his life-changing message. The same is true for the rest of the Bible. On each page we can learn new things about God and how He wants to interact with us.

I hope that the few short stories that I've been able to share have helped you to consider the reality of Jesus seriously. If you need more convincing then don't stop here. You probably have a Bible in your house. It is still the most bought, if not the most read, book in the world. It's available on the internet, on Kindle, on your iPhone and is still making its presence felt in most hotels, hospitals and prisons. Pick up a copy and start reading. As you do, ask God to show Himself to you and to send His Holy Spirit so that you can see Jesus clearly on every page.

If you don't need more convincing then it's time to make a change. It's time to start a new life with Jesus at the centre, enjoying the ultimate relationship, the relationship that you were created for in the first place. If this is something that you want to do, then the following prayer is a great place to start.

Father God,
Thank you for sending Jesus into the world to meet with people like me. Thank you that he died in my place to forgive the wrong things I have done so that I can be in a relationship with you again. I want to confess with my mouth the things that I believe in my heart, that Jesus is Lord. Please send your Holy Spirit to be in my life to change me for the better so that I can learn to follow you from this day onwards. Amen

If you have prayed this prayer then do let me know. You can email me at ed@gileadbookspublishing.com or scan the QR code on the back cover to visit The Bad Samaritan website.